MEDIA SECRETS REVEALED

Lori McNeil

Published by Prominence Publishing,
www.prominencepublishing.com

Media Secrets Revealed/ Lori McNeil. -- 1st ed.
ISBN 978-1-988925-40-0

CONTENTS

Introduction

Imagine a world where you have the power to tap into relevant media exposure for you and your business. Well, it does exist. There are so many amazing and untapped opportunities out there. Each of us desire to increase our media exposure, build our brands, build our presence and communicate those important messages for greater impact. They're out there and as a business coach and educator for over 20 years, I have worked with many people that struggle achieving media goals as well as understanding how to leverage it for maximum impact. I remember as a young girl fantasizing about Hollywood stars, actors and actresses that at the time seemed untouchable. There was something magical about flipping through magazines, watching different television programs and commercials just thinking that these people must have the most amazing life. They had it all. There were magical. As a kid you idolize different people and look up to them. I think now as an adult, there are certain people in the spotlight who seem to get more attention – everybody knows their name. Remember Norm from cheers? They walk in the door and everybody says hello.

Norm represents what is true in Hollywood. Certain people are known and loved more, not necessarily because they are ideal, but because they show up. Even growing up I idolized different people in Hollywood for different reasons, whether I thought they were cute, and I had a crush on, somebody who's beautiful, or that couple who appear to be a dynamite power couple and they portray the perfect life. It doesn't matter what it is. There's something that seems untouchable about certain people. Maybe you've met them. Maybe you've never had the opportunity to attend an event or had an opportunity where you could meet them face to face. They seem out of reach yet so close. In some ways this can be good as it pushes us to be better. Oftentimes, it seems like we will never measure up.

This is the tricky element about media. When someone runs a great marketing, branding, or media campaign, it can appear that everything is great. The older that we get the more that we realize that there's no such thing as a perfect life, perfect person, a perfect family, or perfect kids. That is not realistic. It is interesting how things can seem that way, right? As I grew older and created the company I have today, I realize that you don't have to be perfect. In fact, it's much better and much healthier for you, not to mention much better for your brand if you're not fake. And if you're being completely authentic about who you are, what you stand for, and what your goals are you become real with people. Norm becomes the fallacy (sorry, George Wendt – I really do love your character).

As culture and technology has advanced, we, as a culture, need to shift how we view Hollywood, how we view media opportunities, and how we view the lifestyle. It is no longer an entity that once seemed untouchable. There is something about media that will (and should) always seem magical. Media has become so much more accessible to us than ever through the advancement of culture and technology. I believe it's important as entrepreneurs, world changers, and influencers that we learn to capitalize on the opportunity technology has for us to reach our target audience. We can now reach people that we would have never had an opportunity to reach 20, 30, 40, or 50 years ago! At least not in the same way or with the same depth. I challenge you to think about the power of media today, and the myriad of ways that now exist, including the differences between perception and reality and how that has shifted in our culture. Ask what you are doing to shift along with it.

There is so much power in media and media is so accessible in so many unique ways that people want to first know that you are real and authentic. They want to be able to meet face to face, to engage emotionally, a real heart connection. Even technology allows people to connect more than ever before. There was once a time when you would see someone (celebrity status) on TV and perhaps in a print magazine. That was the extent of connection unless you were the lucky few who were invited to a special event where you feasibly could meet them or shake their hand or be within a thousand feet of them. Flip the script and now, there's YouTube, Facebook, Instagram, and various other social media platforms to connect with your audience other than "as seen on TV' and that's amazing shift.

Then how does that work with engaging your audience through media. There are five main strategies that I have used personally for years that have worked. I have a

100% success rate on every single pitch I have ever made. I am confident in my results. Depending on your own goals, this process may or may not be exactly the path you take however, if you are reading this, you have my full blessing to implement the process into your own journey because I live the results.

PART ONE

Preparing Your Mindset

"By failing to prepare, you are preparing to fail."
—Benjamin Franklin

There are a myriad of strategies relating to media exposure like how to pitch yourself and how to obtain decent results. What I'm not saying is that this is the only way to pitch or this is the only way to be successful. What I am saying is that my simple process gets results and has for many years without being complicated. Let's break down my five-step strategy process as well as strategies to consider.

This may seem a little bit simplistic at first (ironically, the whole five step process is not difficult), yet an interesting point to note is that many entrepreneurs neglect to implement some of the most basic concepts needed to be successful. Resist the urge to ask, "where's the magic in this?" Truth is, when you implement the fundamentals, those basic concepts, success comes knocking. Keep that in mind as you're going through this process. Take the time to write notes and delve deeper into each strategy. Allow your creativity to flow more. Allow yourself those "a-ha" moments to think a differently than you have up to this point. Have you been playing the "doing the same things and expecting different results" game? If your current strategies were effective, this book would not be in your hands right now. Even if the strategies are something you have tried, use this book to think about little tweaks and changes you can make to implement the strategy better.

 SECRET MEDIA TIP: SIMPLICITY IS NOT A NOVICE MOVE

We are just beginning to scratch the surface here. Learning or implementing these five strategies will yield zero results unless you have prepared your mind first. Mindset births strategy. Strategy paves the road to success and exposure. It's one thing when your audience sees you in a print magazine, which is amazing. However, that's just one aspect of your media campaign. Never forget the advancement of technology and the various ways that media can be utilized for greater impact. Long gone are the days where media was almost out of reach and only for those whom were considered successful (a household name... remember Norm?). Now, it is sprinkled as pieces into an overall business strategy. Things have evolved so much that you must incorporate a media strategy into your business plan. Integration is critical.

One of the biggest mistakes I see is people do not take the time to understand the world of media. For many, it's still viewed as this extra thing, kind of floating out in space a bit. The belief that if you have a little bit of extra time and if you have a little bit of extra-extra money then you can look at doing something media related. The truth is that you're missing the boat. Entrepreneurs that fail to understand the full spectrum of media – how it works – how to leverage aspects and avenues using the various technology are literally leaving money on the table. Entrepreneurs need to think about their business planning and their media strategy plan as one. Once you dissect the details of each one, especially if you are used to thinking of them as two separate concepts consider having two plans side by side so that you can see the overlap, you can figure out how the pieces fit together.

Many entrepreneurs out there do not have an actual written business plan. If they do, they do not refer to it regularly or see it as it really was designed to be – a living, breathing daily document. The same rings true for media plans. Your media plans should be a living, breathing document used daily and the two should not be mutually exclusive. They are most effective when developed together for fleshing out or brainstorming purposes to get ideas, concepts, strategies down on paper. That should be part of the development process. Eventually they need to one living breathing document because all your strategies when interwoven together will find their flow and work continuously. I see so many entrepreneurs not understanding how this fits together which is why I wrote this book. I am extremely passionate about teaching people the foundations of business and overall business strategies to become successful. Deeper still, I'm passionate about teaching people how their media strategies and their media plan & vision fit into their overall vision itself. This is the essence of creating a legacy for your business.

Media is an amazing tool that can fast track your success if structured correctly. If you fail to structure it correctly and sporadically utilize media, maybe throw a little bit of time and money at it occasionally, you will not see the results, you will not see the Return in Investment (ROI). When you don't see the results and you don't see the ROI, you won't see it's worth. It is worth it. I talk to people all the time who, because they don't see the ROI don't think that certain media strategies are worth the time and money and it's often because they're not implementing a well-rounded strategy. Typically, they are not even implementing any strategy into their overall business vision and business planning. This is something I really want you to take seriously. Dive into these strategies, uncover the nuggets, go deep and do the hard work. The rewards are there.

You must complete the foundational work and that takes time. Often it is not the fun piece for many entrepreneurs. They think that they can skip over this part, think about it jot down a few notes and it will flow. You really must spend some time purposely developing and flushing out documents that don't just sit on your shelf but that intrinsically become a part of you. You wrote it. You breathe it. You live it. *Every. Single. Day.*

The Other Side

Of course, there is the other side which is tracking results. You should be keeping track of your numbers, not just the financials but tracking all your data. One of the best ways to track is to have an implementation plan that is a part of your overall business plan. When you develop that business plan and that media plan and you integrate those and you interweave those and they are become one document, you can simply track every aspect of plan not just winging or guessing and thinking 'oh, I had a great day today, or I had a great week, or I had a great month' but you'll actually have data in front of you that proves your numbers which can determine the success of certain strategies as well as strategies that need to be tweaked. Here is the pivot. Continue to dig deep into answering the question why? Why did that strategy not work? Why was I not as successful in implementing a certain strategy when I thought that it was a rock star idea or a rock star strategy? You can't keep doing the same thing expecting a different result. This is the hard work, that when diligently pursued yield amazing results.

SECRET MEDIA TIP: YOU CAN CHANGE THE STRATEGY, BUT YOU NEVER CHANGE THE GOAL.

You have an ultimate vision burning within you. That ultimate desire that requires your continual persistence. It's okay to pivot. It's okay to change the strategy, but you should never change the goal. So many people that I talk to get confused thinking that because they've been spinning their wheels working so hard that their goal must not be realistic, or they become confused about whether that's the right goal to have. I will tell you that if something is burning within you, especially entrepreneurs who have visions and huge goals, don't change the goal. That burning desire within you IS the goal. It is a part of you and who you are. As you develop your business plan and move forward with that remember to track your results. Tracking your data, having the numbers in front of you helps you make the best decisions to develop the best strategies needed to reach those goals. Remember:

- ✓ It is okay to change the strategy – not the goal.
- ✓ It is okay to change the strategy – not your ultimate vision.

This is something I want to caution you against. If you have certain media goals, if you have certain media strategies, you must ensure that you have the right strategies that fit that goal and you need to start somewhere – act. Know you may need to pivot and change the strategies in order to meet your ultimate goal. If you have a specific goal of being on a specific show or featured in a specific media outlet be aware of the goals and strategies needed on all levels and stay on top of what is working and not working so that you can pivot when needed in order to reach your ultimate vision – that destination for your business, for your life.

Remember, when you're so focused in one direction on something you're not allowing the space needed for the things in your life, the things in your business that are waiting out there for you. I see this happening so much. You may have to pivot. Stay aware. You can pivot the strategy. Don't change the goal. Be persistent about achieving your goals. Do not think if you stay persistent in a strategy that you're making a good decision in staying the course. This is where confusion sets in. It's okay. It's okay to give up the strategy. Don't give up the goal. Understand how all of these pieces fit together and be willing to walk away from strategies (even if that means money you've spent and sometimes a lot of hard work and a lot of time and a lot of grief and a lot of frustration and a lot of sacrifice) in order to ultimately meet your goal and to not hang onto the negativity and hang onto the things that aren't working. So, let's back up a moment. My experience has been that the simple things, the foundational things, are what work, but are not being done. So, let's start with the first strategy, that of preplanning.

PART TWO

The Strategies

Making the shift from mindset to movement is where the rubber hits the road and is where you will find the greatest success. Mindset without movement will keep you stuck. Movement without mindset will send you off track. Both are important and it is crucial to learn how to mirror the two together. Before you press into the following five strategies that will change how you approach media, take a moment to look back over the previous pages and see if there are actions you need to take to put your mindset in place. Once your mindset is focused, you are ready to digest the strategies. Having the right mindset will allow you to receive the most value from these strategies.

Strategy1: Pre-Planning

"In preparing for battle, I have always found that plans are useless, but planning is indispensable."
- Dwight D. Eisenhower

Pre-Planning is the first strategy in the five- step process and consists of two parts. Consider all the different projects that you are engaged in through the lens of who you are and how you're presenting your-self... even before you type a word or make that phone call and before you make that pitch. There are some critical checkmarks that must be done prior to initial contact. Think about your presence both on and offline. Think about your messaging, the continuity of your messaging, and the clarity of everything through your branding, your communication, to what you're teaching online. This stage in the process matters regardless if your business is online or brick and mortar. The type of business or business structure doesn't matter.

The continuity of your messaging and branding is critical. Media professionals are busy. They are being pitched constantly. Always be thinking about what makes you different. How will your pitch stand out? How is the essence of who you are different from anyone else? Everything starts in the pre planning before you contact anyone. I strongly encourage you to go through all social media platforms, all classes, websites, everything that you've done or doing to this point. First, ensure that your messaging is consistent as well as your visual images. Why?

SECRET MEDIA TIP: USE VARIOUS PLATFORMS TO POLL WHERE PEOPLE ARE FINDING YOU.

Pre-planning is made up of two parts. The first part is knowing and understanding the research that the outlets do on you and to be ready. This was covered in the first part of the book. Now is a good time to take another look at your online presence and make sure it is consistent. The second part of pre-panning is what you do to prepare for researching the outlet and their needs, audience, and the like. Let's look at what the outlets look for first.

Step 1: Their Research

Approximately 85% of the time after my pitch has been accepted and I'm in, either on the show or I'm being featured, the media outlet has already conducted some deep research on me as part of their preparation. I am continually amazed at what they dig up off the Internet from a basic internet search. I have been blessed to be in the media a lot and in most interviews, I have ended up being asked something random regarding information that I did not provide for them. When this happens, I know instantly where that information came from. And not that my messaging is inconsistent, but I know (and so should you) what verbiage, phrases and photos I use on the various platforms. The messaging is consistent, yet the verbiage be different. If you know your own stuff, it becomes an easy way to decipher where they got that information. That's another little secret: know your own stuff – it'll save you. Once, on an international radio show with 3.5 million listeners, the information that I pitched and provided to the producer was slightly different than the info used to introduced me during the show. I knew immediately that some of the information that the host used came from another source (this one, LinkedIn). Again, the messaging was the same, but the wording slightly different. This information was obtained by the outlet during their pre-planning for that show.

Here's another way to think about this process. It is like applying for a job. We have all heard that your resume gets you the interview and the interview gets you the job. Likewise. being featured in media is like the "job" you are trying to get, and your pitch is the resume that get you in the door. Pre-planning is part of what gets you on their radar to decipher if your interesting enough to benefit their audience. That is why this process is so important. The outlet is also going to Google search you. They will research what's 'out there' about you, whether it's your website, your social platforms, that newspaper article that come up in Google... whatever it is, they're going to find out as much about their guests as possible and they may pull different questions from what they find or like what happened to me on that international show, you may be introduced a little bit differently than what was originally provided. This step in the process must not be overlooked.

Beyond that, the outlet will want to know how active you are. How engaged you are. How passionate you are about your cause across the board. Are you consistent? Are you going to make a good guest? Are you going to add value to the show, or are you just simply wanting to be on TV for the sake of being on TV? They want people that are super serious and super passionate. It doesn't matter if your show is booked out a few weeks, or a few months, or even if it is a year away, they're still going to be watching you and your activity. They're going to watch how your followers respond to you. How your readership responds to you. Are you engaged in follow ups on social media threads for instance? They're going to do their due diligence to ensure that you will be a quality guests and how you interact with people and the language that you use and how you answer questions (verbally or written) will all come into play.

You're not necessarily going to respond with lengthy answers to every question on your social media sites, but your overall messaging should be consistent. They want to know that you are interesting and engaging. You may have a great website because somebody designed it for you and is helping you with your branding. That's great. They still want to know about you. So how are you personally interacting and engaging with your audience? Therefore, the pre planning process is incredibly important. Again, the basics.

As previously mentioned, only about 85% really dig deep before I go onto a show. The other 15% might do something quick. This has happened to me on radio, podcasts, and TV, maybe because they were running just a one or two-person operation, so their research time might have been limited. In cases like that the outlet relied completely on me to provide the information they needed as they may or may not have had time to do additional research. The other reason this happens within that 15% is that things in media move very, very quickly. They may have changes in their schedule, changes in their guest appearance schedule, or maybe somebody canceled on them. You may even get asked to be bumped up. If that happens, then they may not have time to fully research you. The world of media runs very quickly therefore you just need to make sure that your messaging in your pitch is very clear and that you are providing enough information that if for whatever reason, they do not have time to do deeper research on you, they have enough information from what you provide to be prepared to ask you intelligent questions and facilitate a solid interview.

SECRET MEDIA TIP: YOU WANT TO INCREASE THE CHANCES FOR ENGAGEMENT DURING THE PRE-PLANNING PROCESS.

It is imperative to know what other messaging, other activities, volunteer work and the like that you have out there on Google as it could be very likely that you get a question you're not expecting. The more you are aware of what's out there, what you're doing, and how people respond to you, the more prepared you will be for questions, even random questions that might not have anything to do with the topic you pitched. That's why this pre-planning process is so important. If you're prepared. If you are interesting enough. You will get the spot. Still, if it doesn't happen don't take it personal. Sometimes it has nothing to do with you. That's why you've got to ensure that all your ducks are in a row. Remember, with all branding, all messaging, all your interactions, and everything across the board can and may be brought up during an interview outside of what you provide for them. Stay aware. This is the first part of pre-planning. The second part is about your research on the media outlet.

Step 2: YOUR Research

The second part is all about your researching the media outlet. Your purpose must be more than just wanting to be on TV or to be featured in a large named magazine. You've got to really prove that you have a purpose, that it's not just about you, and that it's not just about you trying to be famous. Unfortunately, there are a lot of people whose main goal is just that. So, you need to be very specific with how you are researching the outlet, how you are communicating, how you will provide value to that outlet and to their audience. Yet, those are two different things. In other words, the way that you provide value to the outlet is different than the value that you add to their audience.

Obviously, the outlet cares deeply about their value brought to their audience. They care about their numbers, their stats. However, there are ways that you can add value directly to the host and producers, directly to the company, or the media outlet. This comes in the form of research. The more research you do on the actual hosts, the anchors, the people that are interviewing you with, producers, and the media outlet itself (whether visual or written) the better. The greater the preparation before that interview takes place, the greater comfort you will have. This process benefits you in your pitch as well as your confidence and comfort during an interview.

SECRET MEDIA TIP: DON'T PITCH TO JUST ANY OUTLET.

Do research. Find out what's going on in that local market, for that outlet. For instance, you don't want to just pitch to anybody and everybody, you want to be intentional with your avatar and the market you're trying to reach. You want to be certain that a publication or television station is a good fit for your audience and for getting your message out. Let's say it's a television interview and you're traveling or flying to a different location, or, maybe it's a local location and you haven't been to that location before, you'll want to know exactly what's important to that station. Every media outlet has a certain focuses or specific causes they like to support. Perhaps there are specific partnerships in that local community they tend to support a little bit more or that are important to that outlet. Maybe they have a partnership with a school and consequently have more features on youth or on education. Your job is to find out what that is or even what's important to the producer, or the hosts, or the first people interviewing you. That is going to be incredibly beneficial for you not only to make your pitch, but when you interact with anyone related to that outlet. You will feel prepared and confident.

Another important part to remember is strategy needs to also include your physical local media. Most people are trying to fast track their success attempting to gain exposure to those higher, more recognized outlets as soon as possible. I can tell you that the fastest way to meet that goal is to actually think about the foundation for your overall media strategy, which is to start smaller in order to build your credibility on your local level, develop your following, practice being interviewed, practice the types of questions that you're going to get asked, and practice your answers over and over and over. This is just something that is an important foundational piece to building your media strategy plan and to getting stronger in media thus solidifying your foundation from the very beginning. This foundation you build must also continually be cultivated. In other words, as your media strategies and goals get bigger and bigger and bigger you need to stay in your local newspaper. You need to stay on your local radio station. This shows the bigger outlets that you care enough to remain involved in your local community. Plus, you don't want your local community to think that you've abandoned them just because you are now a 'celebrity' or a bigger business with a bigger vision or a bigger brand that has 'outgrown' what you've built locally and have been successful with. On a larger scale they want to be happy for you. You want to keep them your cheerleaders. You don't want to abandon them when you outgrow the local market, nor do you want them to feel like you've outgrown them. Staying involved gives you backing, support, and maintains your credibility when the naysayers come out of the wall (and they will).

Your immediate strategy plan begins to shift a little bit to be multi-dimensional. It is an important aspect to remember There are different reasons around being involved in your local media outlets and it will help you achieve long term goals faster by maintaining that local foundation as part of your overall media strategy plan. The bonus is that they will continue to give you all kinds of content. If you are working toward pitching bigger outlets, whether print, media, television, radio, doesn't matter, credibility counts. You are building your credibility online while practicing at home in your local media outlet. It's a building process and it's a very important piece that more entrepreneurs need to understand and grasp onto. Your local market gives you advantage more than you realize.

Learning Your Surroundings

Another critical element to find out is the setting in the studio. Whether a small or larger studio you'll need to know what the colors are. You want to show up wearing complementary colors that will help you stand out. For TV, wear simple, plain, bright colors. Not fluorescent, but vibrant colors that stand out, yet do not distract others from your content or the reason you are there.

SECRET MEDIA TIP: SIMPLICITY IS BEST.

Many people are not aware that colors can come across different on TV than what is seen in person. For instance, I was in Utah doing a live TV interview and the top half of my dress was dark Fuchsia, however you couldn't tell that on TV. When you look at the photos or watch the footage, the top half of my dress looks red. My branding colors are a combination of magenta and fuchsia. I was wearing a dress that was a bit lighter shade of pink on the bottom and a darker color on top, although on camera it ended up looking red. Unfortunately, the interview couch I was sitting on was also red and I think that really pulled those red hues out of that dark magenta even more than I expected. What saved me was the color of my skirt was a different color which helped me to 'pop' from that bright red couch even more. Happy that my entire dress was not darker magenta as I would have blended in way too much. A perfect example of why you need to do research on set colors. Get on the media outlets website and research the actual sets. You can access this from footage and photos of previous shows. Make sure that your colors are going to be complementary and that you're not going to blend in too much. Sometimes it's last minute and you don't have time for this type of research. Do the best you can. If time allows, I highly suggest this. Not enough people are doing this and when I see people on TV, on camera, the footage afterwards; I can see the simple fixes that a little research would have prevented. This is crucial for both men and women.

Men, your wardrobe should consist of either brown or black shoes and a simple tie that doesn't have too much color or design unless it is specific to your branding. Ladies, you want to keep your shoes neutral. I suggest either nude or a black, something very simple. You don't want something on TV that looks beautiful or amazing in person as it comes across differently. I would suggest staying away from bright flashy shoes unless, like a mans tie, it specifically corelates with the essence of who you are or your brand. Keep your jewelry very simple. Stay away from chunky jewelry with your necklaces or too flashy of earrings (unless again that is your branding). You want to make sure that any embroidery or design you might have on your shirt, on your blouse or on the upper part of your dress is very simple. Remember, wrong colors and patterns can be very distracting more than you realize. And, always bring a back-up wardrobe just in case! You never know when you might tear something or spill something! Finally, I would avoid too many earth tones as they just don't show up well on camera. Green tones can show up well but steer clear from browns. Now, an exception is that sometimes black can show up on camera well (provided the actual set doesn't have too much black). Pay attention to what the hosts typically wear. Obviously, you don't know what they're going to wear, but if you watch enough clips, you can figure out what their style might be or how that they might dress so that you can be complementary to your hosts (which subconsciously to the host adds value).

You may be thinking this is a whole bunch of research! This is crazy! Who does this? Exactly. That's my point. There are not enough people who spend the time doing this. You can squander time in this process researching however, the reality is that it doesn't take very long. If you spend even 10 or 15 minutes researching on their website and just getting an idea of what their stages look like, what their sets look like, maybe watching a couple of the clips, or going to their Facebook page. Practically every media outlet has their own Facebook page or own social media platforms. This is valuable information you can obtain quickly. Most media outlets have one studio TV set and many of the bigger stations have two or three. Don't feel overwhelmed with this process. A little bit of information can be so powerful and provide so much value for you and help you be prepared. Keep in mind that this may seem like preparation. It's not. The process of the preparation phase is different. We will get to preparation later in the book.

Strategy2:
The Pitch

"I am sorry for such a long letter, I didn't have time
to write a short one."
-Mark Twain

T he second stage in the five-step strategy process is the pitch. Your pitch should include four separate, yet connected sections. Many pitches are not being prepared correctly. I see awful things to be honest. Let's first talk about how not to pitch. There are three avenues you should not take regarding your initial relationship connection and/or your first pitch to that outlet. If you are doing any of these, I want you to stop right now. Don't do these things. First, do not contact someone in a Facebook direct message unless the relationship has already been established in some way and it has been communicated that it is an acceptable way to contact them. This might work in a small community if you're living in it and it's your own local market. Still, not the most professional way to start the relationship, if you're active in your local community, you might be known already. There are times then, when that that might be okay, but not as an initial pitch or for initial contact. I see a lot of people doing this. Facebook is a great tool, but it's not a way to make an official pitch or make even an initial introduction. In other words, don't contact media in the same way you would a friend or random connection on social media. It is for after you've established the relationship, but not initially. Keep that in mind.

SECRET MEDIA TIP: MAKE SURE YOU KNOW WHAT NOT TO DO!

Another thing I see that you should steer away from is trying to build the relationship through a cold email. Media outlets are very busy, they get thousands of pitches on a regular basis. Don't try to build the relationship through email. They want to know the value you bring; they want you to get to the point. You're building a relationship, but you're not wasting their time. Don't go back and forth with a ton of emails. It will create a time-wasting portal that often leads to nowhere.

Cold calling is the third mistake I see a lot. Calling an outlet can be incorporated as part of your overall strategy once the relationship has been established, but do not call an outlet using a cold call for an initial contact. Those are among the main mistakes that I see when people are trying to establish that initial relationship or initial pitch. Again, these are specific examples of what NOT to do!

Now we're going to be talking about things that you want to do when building relationships with media and making successful pitches.

What a Successful Pitch Looks Like

We are ready to dive into what the pitch consists of. In your pre-planning, you've already done your research, you already know the names of the producer, you already know the names of your hosts or your possible hosts. Now, you need to at least know who the regular host of the segment that you're pitching, whether it's a newspaper, a magazine, radio, or TV. Remember, there are different sections, segments, and shows. For example, make sure that you're pitching to a specific show, not just to the

network overall. There are different hosts, writers, producers and editors or each specific segment. Make sure you know which people you need to be communicating with and building relationships with, in order to accomplish your goals.

Whenever I make a pitch, there is a specific strategy not many utilize effectively – send it to more than one person. Don't just send it to the producer or editor. Research the names and direct email addresses for several people. You want the exact email addresses. I find the people in charge of making decisions. Whenever I make a pitch, I will pitch at least two to three people; I will "cc" all of them on the same email. It doesn't matter if it's a speaking event on a stage or a media appearance; this is how I pitch. This will often change once specific relationships have been built and contacts established. Send your initial pitch to more than one person because you never know the influence that each person might have, the personal interest that each of those people might have in order to be an advocate for you. Never make assumptions about personal interests. The brainstorming will automatically be so much smoother when you send it to more than one person. You will potentially eliminate one person having to go to other people and explain to them what they've just read in your email or expecting them to take the extra time to forward the email to other decision makers.

SECRET MEDIA TIP: WHEN YOUR STRATEGY WORKS... PERFECT IT.

This strategy is a contributing factor in my success rate. Pay close attention to the smallest details within this process. There is so much power in each aspect and sometimes all it takes is a minor tweak or two that will catapult your success. Once you are ready to write and deliver your actual pitch, you're not giving your elevator pitch. Many people try to spew all kinds of information about themselves to sound impressive enough that media outlets can't say no. At least that's the rationale used. You'll want to be very, very specific about introducing yourself.

After a brief introduction, I have different ways that I phrase the value that I'm bringing to their audience. Because that's part of my messaging and my pitch, I tailor it just a bit different once I've done my pre-planning and I research. The value section of your pitch should only be a couple of sentences. You're not going into this whole big spiel about yourself and about everything that you do and everything that you offer. You want to make sure that the email has white space. You're not sending them an exhaustive letter. Another mistake I see way to often. What you want to do is lead with value and provide only the most important information. Keep the paragraphs short or use bullet points. They're busy. You just want to send them quick snapshots. They want to know: who are you; what do you offer; what's the value to their audience; what do you want to speak about; and what are your speaking points. Keep everything simple. Once you've done a couple of sentences of your intro, make sure you have white space, then talk briefly about the value you bring, not the services that you offer - not your products that you offer - but the value of what you offer. This is your second little paragraph.

 SECRET MEDIA TIP: VALUE IS VALUABLE.

I add value by including a few highlights that add credibility and authority. Not a laundry list Not a resume. Specific, brief, and powerful. One thing I pitch is my book series teaching literacy skills. If I'm making a pitch on National Family Literacy Day, that's going to be the focus of my pitch. It's not going to be my Legacy Builders program. It's not going to be anything about Media Secrets or me a speaker or coach. I'm going to stay focused on the value of literacy, the results of specific strategies, and the value of why that's important. My second paragraph might say something like, "I am a bestselling author of a 10 books series focusing on 5 specific strategies proven in increase literacy skills." Along with this, I might also add, "I just got back from Washington DC where I was a guest of the presidential Bush family and I raised 3.5 million dollars nationally for literacy." Can you see how this elevates my credibility but also adds value? Outlets want to know that you are active in your cause and getting results. They want to see one solid example, which is why I mention Washington DC and the value that I brought that platform. Don't waste time or space. Only three or four sentences and a little bit about what you are doing currently. Not what you did last year, not what you've done 10 years ago, but currently, and they love knowing if you've had any kind of exposure experience. If you haven't, it's not a check mark against you, but if you have anything you can leverage (written in your local paper, featured some way, or been involved in a cause in your community) then utilize it. Don't worry if there were only 50 people in the room, use something showing you are active in your messaging, active in your cause, mention it briefly and the value or the result of you being involved in that furthered the cause. This is the second part of your pitch when adding value. Again, this is either a couple bullet points or a couple of sentences.

In the third section of your pitch, now you're including more specific talking points. When I pitch my 10- book series on literacy, this is where I add more specific supporting information. I may say, "my 10 book children's series is unique because it teaches five specific literacy strategies that teach kids literacy skills within the storyline itself. No other book out there does this." I might add a couple more sentences, maybe even a couple of bullet points to highlight certain strategies like "I look forward to adding value to your audience as we work together to increase literacy skills globally" or something similar. Each time it is a little different. You are already planting the idea in your mind that you are so confident over what you have to offer, your messaging, your strategies, your program, your book, whatever it is that you are confident in expecting to hear from them. Focus on Neuro Linguistic Programming (NLP) in that bottom part. If you aren't familiar with NLP, take some time learning the basics. NLP will help you communicate your messaging with greater clarity as well as help you make stronger pitches. These are the three main sections of your pitch, and each section should be succinct and short with lots of white space.

The fourth and final section is your salutation and contact info. Be sure and include your website, social media sites, email address and anywhere else the can find you easily that supports your pitch. If you have other sites that are not directly related to the pitch, such as another business, do not include them. Make it very easy for the outlet to research you. Include all this type of information at the bottom. I don't use my phone number because I prefer everything in writing as you don't have to remember details discussed via phone if everything is in writing. You decide whether you want to include a phone number. I have found this very beneficial on multiple occasions.

SECRET MEDIA TIP: THERE ARE TWO MAIN STRATEGIES USED TO PITCH SUCCESSFULLY.

A second way to pitch is with more of a visual impact. Depending on the goals you're trying to accomplish in the messaging, you may want to use this way. If you want to be a little more visual (and we live in a very visual society), you'll need to design a professional 'One Sheet.'

Design your One Sheet super simple but with very specific information. Take the components just covered and put them in quadrants in a graphically pleasing design. This isn't a 'two- page resume.' You're not trying to create a pdf workbook document to show everything under the sun about you. This is literally one page, one sheet. If you have specific branding colors, which I highly, highly suggest, this is where you want to feature those colors and logo that supports the messaging you want to use. Take the four sections discussed and design four quadrants. It is imperative that this One Sheet is designed professionally. If you do not have design skills, hire a professional. Do not attempt to design this yourself.

Our natural eye movement reads from an upper left diagonally down to bottom right. That's just the natural flow of when we look at or read something; a newspaper, a photograph, doesn't matter, unless there's something that's just popping out at us that our eye is drawn to at a different location on the page. Sometimes this can be intentional. The rationale for this would be to create a pattern interrupt and use NLP in a more visual way. Therefore, your logo, branding, photo, etc... should be in the upper left corner of your One Sheet. As you design each quadrant, think about the zigzag of how the natural eye pattern ends up in the bottom right, where your contact info should be. And that's the contact. You have all the same information, however in a very graphically pleasing pitch. If you have the software or the ability to include it in the email text itself...perfect. If not, a PDF attachment is suitable and industry acceptable. Then you recap just a little bit in the text of the email itself because you want to give them a reason to open that document. You want to offer enough information to get them to click on that pdf to learn a little bit more. The messaging is same but, but it's not redundant. This is where you might include a powerful statistic or something cool that that elevates you, causing the reader to react with "wow, that's interesting."

If your One Sheet is full color, still maintain a good deal of white space on the page and not too cluttered (which tends to happen when creating visuals). Use that concept of bulleted points and a lot of space in the different quadrants. Not sure which of the two different pitch types you need, go ahead and split test and use both. For instance, if you want to pitch to two national television networks and you're on the fence trying to decide like which way to pitch, whether it's strictly email or a designed One Sheet, you can split test it to see what is getting you the greatest response. I can tell you that if your pitch is good and your value is valuable, you should hear back from most media outlets within a few days. It doesn't take that long to get a response. However, if you don't hear back within a week to 10 days, it could be something that doesn't relate to you. Perhaps the decision maker is on vacation or busy. Maybe the segments are already booked out several weeks or months. Remember not to take anything personally. If you get a rejection notice, learn from it and move on. Sometimes I have media outlets that will contact me a second time or at the last minute because I'm someone that's in their hopper. Don't get discouraged, you never know how things will evolve and what opportunities will pop up unexpectedly. If you are contacted last minute, figure out a way to make it work. This happens with newspaper stories and radio interviews quite frequently.

Once you've made your pitch and your pitch gets accepted, you immediately want to thank them and ask a few logistical questions especially if they have not provided enough information for you. Don't overwhelm them. Don't ask a ton of questions that make it seem like you haven't done your research (Strategy 1) or give them reason to believe that you will be a pain to work with. Ask only a few specific questions. This shows engagement, credibility, and builds the relationship. If you're waiting for their response and your kind of wondering what's going on, do a follow up with them. Once you've done the follow up, wait. You are not just pitching to one outlet and waiting. Don't put all your eggs in one basket, but don't blindly send pitches everywhere. Practice your pitches and tweak your pitches. Split test this a little bit. Go ahead and pitch to at least two or three media outlets at the same time. Remember, you're learning and growing and making tweaks and that's fine. You're trying to fill your calendar and get results as fast as you can. It can be tempting to wait on one pitch before you make the next pitch. Don't do that. That's a mistake that a lot of people make. Go ahead and pitch two or three at the same time and just have this revolving door pitch strategy because media outlets will want to book you 2-3 months out anyway. They more than likely will not book you for next week; may or may not even be that same month. You want to make sure that you're constantly pitching at least two or three because you're booking them two to three months out. Get organized. Create a media schedule and keep track of where each media outlet is so you can follow up accordingly and know exactly where you are in the process with each one. Don't guess, know exactly.

Strategy 3:
Preparation

"Success depends upon previous preparation, and without such preparation there is sure to be failure."
-- Confucious

The next part of the process is preparation. I want you to think about preparation in a different light. This part of the process teaches you to prepare for your interview. The pre-planning part of the process teaches you how to prepare for the pitch. Once your pitch has been accepted, and you have more details about your interview, you are going to know your allotted timeframe. TV spots will be 3-5 minutes and most radio or podcasts range from 30-60 minutes. You need to be incredibly focused and add as much value as possible in a short amount of time. Respect the given time and be especially aware of the time clock. There's usually a time clock countdown somewhere within your line of sight. During the interview, time will go by faster than you think. In preparation for your interview, practice your bullet points and your timing. Be very specific in what you want to communicate in that short amount of time that adds value. Be very strategic in this preparation process. You can't go on and on with examples and stories.

Let's talk about how to best prepare for an interview where you are not live in the studio. In some cases, it might be a national television show and they might use technology where you're still live on the air in a show using technology and video. It's just a different way of being interviewed on that show. Ensure that you are in an aesthetically pleasing room, an office, or a room where there's no distractions and is nicely decorated. You want to make sure that you do not have a door anywhere in your shot. This is a mistake that a lot of people make because especially with the increase of technology and mobility, there's a lot of people have home offices. There's nothing wrong with that, but you do not want a door behind you. A window is okay because that communicates opportunity and positivity. The door creates a negative feature in a shot. If you are live video of any kind be aware of your surroundings. You really want to make sure that you have a great lighting. Lighting is super important. These are all things that you want to make sure are set up and tested way in advance. You want to test your technology in advance. You want to make sure that you have a good camera set up. You want to test your microphone. You might have a headset, or a nice mic set up that would be included in the shot. Keep these in mind when you're interviews as a lot more media outlets are utilizing technology and not physically in a studio anymore. I co-host a show where this is the case. I can tell you what makes a lot of difference when you give time and thought to your background, whether there's a door behind you, whether your decorations or your room are too distracting or cluttered. Make sure that you have depth of field in your shot. You want to make sure that it's quiet but there nothing else going on in the room or just right outside the door, that kind of thing. You want to make sure that you have a good sound system set up. You want to make sure you have excellent lighting, there's a lot of things to consider and you want to make sure that you are ready. You really want to reduce what is seen in your shot. Keep this in mind when you are doing live online or live feed types of interviews.

Many national radio stations still use Skype. People think of Skype as being kind of antiquated, that a lot more people maybe are using Zoom or WebEx or other types of technology. Once you learn what you need set up on your computer and on your system, you want to make sure you test all of that. Specifically, for radio you'll want to make sure that you test your computers bandwidth because if you don't have strong enough bandwidth, screens will freeze, especially if you are animated and it will take away from your performance.

Television has 30 frames per second, which the eye reads as consistent movements. A slow Internet connection only has 10 to 15 frames per second. The eye reads as a separate brain. Therefore, you want to limit your head pans and our movements unless you have a good camera and a fast connection. Skype is the only format in which gesturing it can hurt your performance. Skype doesn't have a very strong bandwidth. Even though there's still a lot of people using Skype at a high level it can be a little frustrating because of looking jumpy when you're speaking. So just something to keep in mind. It doesn't mean that you don't want to accept an opportunity that uses Skype. It just means you want to be very aware of your bandwidth and you want to be very aware of your movements and to make fewer or slower movements to ensure smooth viewing.

I want to add here a bit on the clarity of your message. Keep in mind that a confused mind always says no. Practicing is so important and having specific soundbites, specific examples, specific value points already practiced in your mind and completely nailed down before the interview is so important. This will help you prepare. This will help you stay focused. This will help you eliminate confusion. You do not want your audience to be confused because if they are... they'll tune out. You could lose credibility and your call to action will fall on deaf ears. You want to get to the point, you want to add value as fast as possible in the most interesting way possible.

Sound Bites

One of the best ways to keep focus and to have the audience ready to act is using sound bites. Sound bites are crucial to practice and to understand how they work so that you know best how to use them in any type of an interview. A sound bite is a short answer the media uses from your interview. There are important things that need to be included in your sound soundbites so that if they extract one little piece of your interview, it's powerful. It has strong messaging, it's clear and it represents you and your brand and what you're trying to communicate very well. There are all kinds of sound bites that you need to make sure you include and that you practice until they become not only a part of your interviews, but they really are a part of your overall branding, brand essence, and brand identity.

Sound bites are very short answers at the media will use from your interview. Traditionally it's a bite size portion of sound taken from a larger body of what you said. That's all it is. A lot of people misunderstand sound bites and get confused. There are basically quotes. It's something you said that's been extracted that's then used as a quote in some way that's kind of highlighted as an important part of what you said. Sometimes, especially in the case of print media, they commonly highlight something important that was said and enlarge it on the page. This is referred to as a call out. Go ahead and make some notes, create your own sound bites. Three to five, maybe seven statements that you want to include as part of your messaging and the points that add value to what you are speaking of. There are different ways that you can do this to prepare. You've seen them as clips used on TV news packages, in print that are pulled out as larger bolded quotes, or in radio are audio clips.

You will develop stronger sound bites the more experience you have doing interviews. It's important to understand what they are so that you then can be thinking about the sound bites that someone may want to pull from your messaging. A quick story. One time I was giving a presentation in Hawaii and while I was on the stage,

I had one of the event coordinators quoting me in real live time on their Facebook page. They were pulling out quotes, (sound bites) that I placed very strategically into my messaging that were already a part of my branding. It wasn't something that just came off the top of my head. I included that in specific places in my presentation on purpose. Although it was a presentation done on stage, interviews or no different You're speaking on a different type of a stage. Keep that in mind. What will help you develop specific sound bites is to remember there are several different concepts to keep in mind when you're creating them. In a chat style interview such as a television radio interview, you want your soundbites to be in intriguing, attention grabbing, adding a little bit of sizzle to raise interest level. This will help you get asked back for a second interview which in the media's eyes equates to you being the authority in your industry or on the topic.

Whether you get asked back for a second interview or not (your chances will be increased), you will automatically elevate your credibility with the media outlet when you learn to talk in sound bites and when you develop your sound bites and practice them and place them strategically throughout your interview, you become invaluable.

For instance, you want to speak in absolutes. The media likes people who give answers that are absolute. You want to be specific when you are speaking. The media loves facts (yes, they do). You are the source, you are the authority in your industry. Whatever the messaging you're trying to get across provide facts, specific data, and statistics. You want to be the authority, that go-to person. You want to give examples that further solidify a point. This can be a personal example. This can be a client example. This can be tied to current events, perhaps something on a bigger global scale that might be very well known, but only give examples that solidify a point you are trying to make. Include action words. Many experts agree that action words punch up your interviews and they help you stand out. This will help you create quotable quotes. Action words will automatically help you in your quotes and help that quote be captured as a soundbite.

SECRET MEDIA TIP: RECORD
YOURSELF AS YOU PREPARE.

Develop slow speech. Don't talk too fast. You can't say everything in a single interview (nor should you). Your preparation in the context of being prepared for your interview is vitally important. Videotape yourself. Use an audio recorder or whatever you need to in order to practice a few times. Whatever your given timeframe, use it wisely. Do not fall prey to the misconception of believing that you will sell anything. You will be asked for your website (where you can have an awesome offer – just don't mention it during your interview). On Podcasts and Radio, you may be asked to share a free offer or a low - ticket product or service. Understanding how to use media in order to get more leads, which in turn will result in sales is fundamental. Keep that in mind that you're not going on TV to sell anything unless asked. This will come in the form of questions like; where can people find you or what is your website. Always have a call to action ready to state. Even if the host or the person interviewing you says, what's one last thing that you would like to leave our listeners today. If you are a health coach, you might say, 'I really want to encourage listeners to focus on the first five pounds that they want to lose.' Focus on what they can or need to do today. Don't be over-whelmed by the call to action, simply have one. Even if it's encouraging them to take the next step like going to your website and downloading a free guide or encourag-ing them to go to Amazon right now and buy your book. There needs to be some value added in your call to ac-tion.

Final Preparation Thoughts

Too many entrepreneurs do not understand how to leverage media and when they don't see the immediate ROI often think media is not worth the time investment. WRONG! Media is a powerful tool when used correctly. It can change the entire trajectory of your business for better or worse. Wouldn't you like it to be on the better side?

Your number one goal is to be strategic and to add val-ue to your audience. That's it. The ROI comes from the increased credibility of being on TV, being featured in magazines, newspapers, podcasts and radio. These all build your authority and credibility. Repurposing your content from each media opportunity is also part of your over media strategy. It's important throughout this whole process to also be thinking about the re-purposing strategy and you really want to shoot behind the scenes (BTS) video and photos. This is very important for relationship building, for building your credibility, for building your brand. It goes beyond just making a Facebook post or doing something on social media, but you want to shoot a video when you're in the green room or in your dressing room. That's a great way to get extra bonus points from the media interview. You can pull out your smart phone and talk directly into it. Just a 30 second or one-minute piece adds a lot of credibility to you being on the set, especially when in a studio and then you post it, using their tags. We talk about this under preparation, so when you arrive the day of the performance, you are ready to go with it. All media outlets will have their social media handles that they want you to use. There's usually a sign in the green room or in the dressing room where they are listed. Make sure that you take a photo of them or write them down and then use the exact tags and handles. When you run into a host or someone in the studio take a quick BTS video or photo. You don't want to ambush or bombard them but be aware and take advantage of the opportunity.

You're behind the scenes videos and photos are great exposure for the outlet and great credibility building for you. Some might have rules against outsiders recording on their premises. If so, follow these rules. Be aware. Be respectful. Don't go around with a selfie stick and be obnoxious and annoying, but again leverage the opportunity. If you have your spouse or a friend or a coworker or somebody with you, maybe you're getting ready and kind of going over some notes or doing some last-minute preps and the makeup chair, have them shoot some BTS. Those shots make great behind the scenes footage. Leverage as much as possible, maintaining professionalism always and have fun. Some of the best shows on television are the behind the lives of celebrities (think of VH-1's "Behind The Music" series).

The more prepared you become, the more prepared you will stay. That preparation will keep you alert and ready to stay on your strategic plan, even when asked questions outside of the scope (remember the first strategy). We will explore this in the next strategy. With preparation grasped, let's look at go time.

Strategy4:
Performance

"The best way to be boring is to leave nothing out."
- Voltaire

Y ou are on a stage. Local, national, international. Your performance makes an impact. That impact grows influence. You don't want to be boring. Practicing speaking to yourself or to an empty room or to your camera has its drawbacks. The only energy is the energy you bring. It's hard to not be monotone and focused when you practice. It can be challenging to not be boring. Be mindful of or about your body language. Verbal and nonverbal communication is huge when building relate-ability with your audience. Being relatable (impact), leads to trust (influence), which ultimately leads to sales (income).

With body language being such a huge part of how we communicate, we must learn to leverage that. It really is somewhat of a performance that you are making on TV (ever wonder why reality TV makes an impact?). You must mentally prepare yourself to somewhat perform; to step into the greater essence of who you are. Have you ever been in a theatrical play in school or in your community? If so, think about how you prepare mentally for a role. If not, research some others in your field (I mean what can it hurt to add some connections, leverage your value, and network your way to more greatness). Use your body language to communicate and emphasize certain points. Strong body language helps to elevate your credibility and makes you more engaging and interesting to watch. Three to five minutes goes by so fast, but I guarantee that the viewer will tune out if you're not interesting. If you are interesting; if you're smiling, if you're making eye contact, if you're motioning to them and to the audience and you're engaging, your hosts are going love you because it's going to make interacting with you so much easier, smoother, and more natural and authentic.

You want to be in control of the interview without being controlling. You don't want to take that control away from anyone interviewing you on any platform. They have certain questions that they're wanting to ask because of what they know they know their audience or how they want to direct the answers. Make sure that no matter what you do your performance always tactfully and strategically points back to your messaging and to the points you want to make. It matters not then what the question is, if you practice enough, and interview enough, you will learn how to strategically redirect questions when needed. This is something that most people do poorly. People who do this well are the ones who have practiced it, and you can tell the difference when you're listening. Given that this is one of those tactics that make someone more interesting and good at being interviewed, mastering this elevates your level of expertise exponentially. It's one of those things that on a subconscious level you may or may not even be aware of when you're watching someone. If you get hit with a question that you're not expecting, answer it in a way that elevates your credibility and redirects everything back to the points that you're trying to make. Even if you don't feel confident in your answer, you need to quickly give an answer and how they relate to your specific points.

SECRET MEDIA TIP: Performance takes Preparation (which looks like practice).

When you've practiced this enough, there won't be a question that you'll be asked that you can't relate back to a point you can make to increase your credibility and increase your messaging. Performance takes practice. Even if you have the most off the wall question about something that doesn't seem on topic, if you are engaging and focused on specific those points in your messaging you can pretty much take any topic and turn it right back around (which is controlling the conversation without being controlling). That's why the preparation and the performance strategies of this process are so important.

The better prepared you are, the easier you will able to confidently and inconspicuously turn any conversation into how it benefits you and your business. You will notice that strategies three and four appear to be the least amount discussed yet carry the most weight. This serves as a visual reminder to you, the reader, that some of the most important concepts in business, when kept simple produce the greatest results.

Special Attention Required

With interviews, there are a few things to be careful of. There's a difference between live versus edited interviews. Live interviews can terrify a lot of people because there is a worry of messing up. That's where practice comes into play and everything that we've been talking about to this point. You can't stop in the middle of an interview you can't say, oh shoot, what I meant was... therefore, don't worry about whether you blow it cause you're still going to have the content that you can repurpose no matter how bad of a mistake that you may make. Just make sure that you don't accidentally say something you can't take back. Edited interviews can take on a world of their own, yet you still want to honor the outlets time, so treating all interviews as if they are live, will keep you sharp. It's just better for your own frame of mind, your own preparation. It's just a good habit to get into. It doesn't matter whether it's something's going to be edited, prerecorded, released six months from now. One question you will want to ask the reporter before you begin is whether you can stop if you make a mistake during the interview. If you're doing live to take, you might want to ask them what the protocol is for that. Again, practice as if everything is live. It will force you to really be very clear on your messaging and be very succinct in your answers and overly prepared.

There are three different types of interviews. There's live, live to tape, and edited or prerecorded and completely edited. Almost all print interviews are edited. Radio interviews though, will run shorter clips rather than the full interviews. When it comes to podcasts, most are edited, however they will run the whole interview at least for the first time its delivered. During a podcast (unless it is a livestream) you can usually stop and restart to answer questions if you messed up. The bottom line is to treat every interview as if it is live and remove the mindset that you can redo and redo because it's recorded. It's just better to practice, practice, practice, and be prepared so that you don't have any frustration or regrets.

One big element to be extremely careful of in any interview, whether it's live, live to tape or edited, is certain things that get timestamped. You want to be able to use the footage over and over and over and have it appear timeless. In order to do this, you need to avoid certain phrases during your interview. You do not want to say things referencing specific dates (even saying yesterday or today), or numbers. For example, if you have an 8-part sequence, avoid referring to them in numbers. If the outlet does its 30 second snippet and the listener only here's "number 3" they may connect a negative emotion to it, what is commonly referred to as FOMO (or Fear Of Missing Out).

It's the value of the messaging that's important. And whether you say yesterday, today or tomorrow, really won't even matter. Also avoid using the reporter's name. Many radio and television interviews are conducted by a producer or an off-air reporter and not by the anchor or the correspondent. You'll hear it on the radio or see on the screen. You want to avoid using the person's name. If you're on a national television show and your hosts are Julie and Steve, you don't want to say, "thank you so much for having me, Julia and Steve, it was a pleasure being here." Make it more generic and simply say "thank you so much for having me." This helps keep your message timeless. And it doesn't matter whether your interview is live, live to tape or edited.

Finally, avoid saying in conclusion or in summary. Many teachers will do this. As a former educator for 20 years, I used to do this in my teaching or informal presentations because you want to have an introduction and then the body and then the conclusion. That is how we are taught to write and to format speeches. In an interview you do not want to say in conclusion or in summary, the audience may never hear what came before your summary (remember the interview is often edited) so you're just stating your conclusion. You should just conclude.

Strategy 5: Post-Planning

"Patience, persistence, and perspiration make an unbeatable combination for success."
-Napoleon Hill

The final strategy that creates a continuous loop in this process is post planning. We hear a lot in life and in business that not enough people are following up. Follow up is crucial whether you've gotten the pitch accepted or not, to build that relationship. Follow-up is a key ingredient in post planning. In fact, post planning is so important and goes beyond the concept of just following up or just being polite. Post planning is also a very specific strategy that I use to get asked back and to continue building my credibility and leverage that relationship to build other media opportunities, whether I've been accepted or not. Don't think that the follow up isn't important If your pitch hasn't been accepted. The important piece here is to concentrate on the post planning. Whether you have been on the show, whether you've been featured or whether you've been ignored, don't skip this step!

SECRET MEDIA TIP: A SOLID POST-PLANNING STRATEGY INCREASES YOUR CREDIBILITY.

It's important to thank your host, to thank your producers, to thank everyone that you met while you're on the show. You will meet a lot of people involved in this process. It's not just about the producer. It's not just about the host or editor. There are others behind the scenes that are vital too. Make sure that you are very gracious and humble with every single person that you meet or cross paths with. Be sure to treat the parking attendants with the same respect as the CEO. This is the essence of credibility. In order to elevate your own credibility, it is imperative to stay in a position of gratefulness for the opportunity across all who are involved in the process. Never treat anyone like they're beneath you. Whenever you meet anyone be very gracious and humble in the process remembering to thank them afterwards, like the security guard who lets you into the set. I can tell you that person possesses mass influence and responsibility. I never leave a building or interview of any kind without completely saying goodbye and thanking absolutely every person that I've met, if they're available. This is important in relationship building. Then after the interview, you want to give them a lot of exposure.

After you leave the building, continue to build the relationship with the outlet. This relationship building will elevate the media outlet as well as elevate your credibility with your own audience. There are many ways you can accomplish this. Posting / re-posting video segments or photos. Shout outs on social media. A blog about your experience. Engaging the outlets other media posts (not just yours that hey may post). The key in this part of the process is to edify the outlet and show gratitude, not use language that edifies yourself. Edifying others will automatically reciprocate itself to edifying you which accomplishes your goal of adding credibility and authority. This is something a lot of entrepreneurs get wrong. Messaging and content creation are important. Don't just make random post of photos and think it's doing much. There needs to be more strategy behind every post. Tag the people that are in the photos as well as any influencers associated with that outlet or interview. DO NOT tag random people! Tag only those which the post pertains to. Every media outlet has specific hashtags. Be sure and find out what they are before you post, so you can use them.

SECRET MEDIA TIP: RECIPROCATE THE RELATIONSHIP WITH AUTHENTIC ENGAGEMENTS.

The strategy behind the Post-Planning allows for the relationship to be reciprocal. When you use hashtags, they put you in front of more people, increasing your reach. It also creates more buzz and activity for the outlet. It's super easy and elevates exposure on both sides. It also allows the outlet permission to use your photos in additional ways if they choose. I have had this happens many times. Never underestimate the power of making everything easy for them. You many need to put in more effort, but the return will pay off ... simply because not many entrepreneurs are taking the time, therefore you stand out. Another strategy that you want to use is sending a handwritten thank you card in the mail. Make it personal. Focus on them, not you. Maybe you remind them of something they did for you while you were there. Something they went above and beyond or something that they said to you when they met you. Be specific. Perhaps it's a personal email and you attach a photo that you took either in front of their station or with their anchors or their hosts or their camera men or something.

These strategies are multi-level. It's not about the basic, "thank you," or being polite, or being professional. Those are the basics of what we do. The sad thing is that so many are not doing the basics, however, when you apply strategies that go above and beyond influential people take notice. Be very strategic and intentional in everything you do. It's not just a matter of sending an email that says, "thank you very much, I enjoyed my time. Let me know if you want me to be on the show again." That is not even an appropriate thank you email to send. Not only is it not personal, and not genuine, it communicates that you truly just wanted to be on their show. Remember all communication needs to be about them not you! It sends the wrong message. You're continuing to build the relationship and add value before you pitch again. With increased trust, perhaps they will reach out to you for additional exposure. I had had this happen a lot with radio interviews and a couple times with newspapers and National TV.

SECRET MEDIA TIP: THINK!

Think about the relationship building both personally and professionally. You're building personal relationships, but you're also building a professional relationship with the network overall. Your strategies need to address both types of relationships. The world of media changes quickly and fast. Producers, camera men, the people that you meet, hosts, anchors that will change stations on a regular basis, oftentimes with little notice. If you've already established relationships with those individuals making another pitch, to a different station and they've moved there, whether you know it or not, your name and that experience is already familiar to them. That's huge.

But What About the 'Bad" interview?

Occasionally you'll have an interview that didn't go well, or you think it didn't go well. Let's talk about that for a moment. When you feel like you haven't done very well in an interview, whether that's a podcast or Facebook live, a national TV show, even a print magazine that you're either writing or it's a piece that you're writing yourself for an outlet that you're being interviewed and featured in, don't beat yourself up because the more you are featured, the more you put yourself out there, the better you will get. That's the first thing I want you to remember. The second thing I want you to remember is that content, no matter how small or big, is a still a huge opportunity. With every media outlet that you're featured in, you can still leverage pieces of that content. Let's say that you were featured in a national TV show and you had a 3- 5 minute national spot and you really don't think it went very well First off, in most cases it went better than you think because we're hard on ourselves. We like to beat ourselves up and we're the most critical of ourselves. The other thing I want you to keep in mind is that because there are so many ways to repurpose content, it doesn't matter how poorly the interview went you can repurpose it. Using the national television show that "you didn't really do that well" in. Okay. Are you still going to have photos from that opportunity? Absolutely. You're still going to have BTS footage from the producers, with the host, in the green room or your dressing room, as well as other various photos that were taken of you during the interview. That's still content. That's still social proof that you can repurpose over and over in a myriad of ways.

Another thing to keep in mind is that you're still going to have the logo to use forever. That goes along with that show. Whether it's a national show or a local circuit show doesn't matter. You still have the credential. You're still going to have that in your portfolio. And just by mentioning it, you've repurposed it. Say that you wore the wrong outfit. It didn't look as good as you thought. Maybe it clashed with the set in some way. Maybe, maybe, maybe, maybe you were stuttering too much. You didn't have very good answers. Perhaps pieces of the interview were just horrible. There are other pieces that can still be used. There are other ways that you can extract that. For instance, you can run the video part, the visual part of your interview without the audio. You can turn that into your own, with your own music and run it as a completely different content that's more visual then it is auditory or again, you add your own music. That adds a different piece of authority to where you have social proof.

You are still being covered in action, but through listening to the interview. As you can see, there are so many ways that you can repurpose that content. Another thing you can do is that from a three to five minutes segment, you should be able to pull out several different 15 or 30 second segments. My guess is that is more, maybe some audio portions to pull from. You need to get creative with some of the content. It's possible because I've done it and I've helped people do it. Don't think that just because you seemingly failed you have powerful assets to use. There is the option to use a voice over. You can rerecord whatever information that you want. You can script out your own question and answer if that's what you want to do and record that and put it into what I call a square audio. You see this allover social media, they're very easy to make. It is your content, your brand, your opportunity. Then you choose whatever photo that you want. Perhaps you were asked a great question, but your answer wasn't good. You script out that question, your own answer, you record that 30 seconds answer and you put your own pieces together. New content. It only takes a few minutes and you've taken content and repurposed it in a completely powerful and legitimate way. Repurposing content is very important. Ask yourself and be very honest, how much content are you repurposing? Many will make a post in excitement like 'I'm going to be featured on a show' and then you might post some behind the scenes photos, within 24 hours after. You send out the thank you post and that's it. Don't let it end there.

 SECRET MEDIA TIP: LISTEN TO ALL YOUR INTERVIEWS

I like to listen to all my interviews. I encourage you to listen to the recordings of all your interviews, whether they're on TV, radio, podcasts, Facebook lives. It doesn't matter what it is, it will help you to listen to your own messaging and know where you need to get better and identify (and fix) any problem areas. Then practice those problematic areas before your next interview. This is where you will really notice the 'ums', the 'likes', the long pauses, or if you're talking too quickly. Perhaps you're interrupting the hosts because you're answering too quickly. You will get better with every single interview. You'll realize a lot when you listen to your own interviews. And even though I have done hundreds of interviews in my career, I still listen to each of them.

One final thought on repurposing your feedback for future use. It's okay to feature something that you did a few months prior, but you do not want to continue reusing the same content delivered in the same way from the same media outlet. You want to make sure that you are being featured in new ways on a regular basis otherwise it's going to devalue you and weaken your credibility. If you do not have a strong enough media strategy plan in place that you are following on a regular basis, your audience is going to see that you're using the same photos, the same video snippets over and over. Don't overuse the same media features without weaving in and adding in new opportunities along the way. It's okay to use old content only if you are continuing to also weave in new content and that is a part of a specific strategy that should be in your overall plan.

Final Thoughts

Think about the ROI on this for just a minute. I've covered a lot of different concepts with this five-step process. There are very specific strategies within every single concept mentioned. If you send out an email and you're not listening to anything I say and you get an interview, great. Good for you. If this is you, I want you to evaluate what opportunities and amount of money you have been leaving on the table because you have not had a specific strategy. This is about the strategy of the long-term goal. Consider the bigger picture. This is deeper thinking that where a lot of people tend to go with this. Be consistently thinking of the higher strategy behind all of this and how you can repurpose content and leverage all the pieces of the process.

Once you reach out, once you make connections and build relationships, you then become that connector and an authority. People will take your suggestions and advice more readily. You may know someone who has a great story or would make a solid guest. Remember, it's not about you. You're helping make that connection for somebody else and continuing to add value to other people. You're elevating your credibility and your relationship with that media outlet, even though you may not be the one being featured. You should be constantly thinking about the process and the ROI. In most cases, you can "pay to play." You can pay to be on TV. You can pay to be on the radio. You can pay to be in a magazine. This option has a different strategy and purpose behind it. Make sure you know and understand the difference. Otherwise, you may choose one option expecting certain results and get frustrated when the results you were after requires another path.

I am not a "pay to play" person. 100% of my pitches come completely organically from building relationships and adding complete value. I have never paid to be on TV ever. There's a certain strategy involved in the "pay to play" options. It's just not the strategy I choose to utilize. Examine how the increased time to learn these deeper strategies can benefit you more holistically as an authority in your niche. The learning curve that you have with media and how the process works will help you make more precise and clearer decisions that affect your entire business. That is why I teach that media strategy must be an integral part of your overall business strategy. The better that you get out the process the more that you step into this process and the more that you learn it, thus the more you grow in accomplishing your goals with media. The more information you obtain about how all this works, even if you choose to a "pay to play" route, your communication and interview skills will grow. I want to encourage you to use strategy when making your decisions. Never allow fear to hold you back. In other words, if you're afraid or having your pitches rejected or you are making excuses for taking the time to learn this process, you are only holding yourself back from deeper levels of success. Don't allow negativity to creep in and affect your decisions.

Everyone wants to maximize their save time. This process isn't time consuming. Does it take time? Is effort involved? Absolutely. Some of the best results come from putting in time and effort. What are your strengths? What are your weaknesses? Where are you dropping the ball? Maybe you are great at pitching, but you're not great at the follow-up. Maybe you're not thinking of the deeper strategy involved in certain aspects. Only you know the truth about what you need to do and what is holding you back. Take a truthful evaluation of your efforts and then take the action needed to change! There may be something within what I shared that you're either not doing or that you could be doing better. Because I've been teaching this strategy long enough to know that there's always something completely missing that's not even on your radar. Maybe you're just dropping the ball and not necessarily doing a great job implementing. Let certain ideas surface with what you're doing or not doing. Ask where you can be doing better in all areas of these five strategies. Remember, within the five strategies there are multiple layers to peel. What are you not doing that you could be doing in order to write a pitch today and have it be accepted? It is entirely possible. You must be very strategic with your process. Very intentional about how you're adding value with every single step of what you just learned. It might take you a little bit of practice of just pitching and refining what works for you, your audience, and your messaging. No matter how successful you are in media, always be working to be better. Strive to be better than you were the day before. Every pitch should be better than the last.

SECRET MEDIA TIP: USE THE
NATIONAL CAMPAIGN CALENDAR AS
PART OF YOUR STRATEGY

I want to share with you one of the best strategies even If you're not good at pitching and you haven't had good success, or if you haven't made your first pitch yet. I'm going to throw out a little secret that will help you. I want you to look at your calendar and I want you to align all the national campaigns and all the national holidays with your messaging. For instance, my main strategy with my children's books and building out legacy is when I have a specific literacy pitch, I look for anything that is connected to with literacy, reading, healthy families, school habits and the like. I use a specific day, month, or week to help bring awareness to support my pitch.

There's a lot of campaigns that can collaborate with schools. I will look at the calendar in advance and be very specific about picking out reading, literacy or education related campaigns that are already on the national calendar. Media outlets love to align themselves with interesting messages that the audience is already going to be interested in based on the national calendar. This is a super easy way to pitch because there are already planned events going on around the globe. It's easy for the media outlet to partner with you and align to support that national campaign with activities and efforts already taking place. Be sure and give the outlet 2-3 months' notice when you pitch using the campaign strategy. Avoid last minute pitches, especially time sensitive campaign pitches. Media outlets need notice.

Work smarter, not harder to align yourself with a specific cause or program that already exists. There are national campaigns for just about everything out there. With a basic internet search, you can get a complete calendar and most of the dates on the calendar have multiple options listed for every day of the year. You might have national Coffee Day with National Wash Your Hands Day, or National Waffle Day with Breast Cancer Awareness Week. How can you get creative with using a calendar that already exists? Easy. It's already given national credibility to some degree in order to make it on the national calendar. When I made my very first TV pitches to national TV outlets, I pitched to ABC and NBC. I used National Family Literacy Day in November to pitch my very first book that I wrote, which has grown into a 10-book series that teaches specific literacy skills within the storyline. If you haven't tried doing this, implement it as a different part of your strategy. If you're scared to make a pitch, it's a simple way for you to make a pitch. Media outlets are looking for stories. They're looking for value and they're looking for interesting people and angles. You've got to be interesting. That's why being interesting is part of the Pre-Planning strategy of the process. Anything that you can do to be interesting, to add value, to be creative, to be different, will benefit them and you is going to be a win/win. Constantly be thinking about how that partnership can be a win/win. Outlets are not just doing you a favor by having you be on TV. They also are looking for interesting stories. Win/win. When your pitch gets accepted, you have shown something of value to them. Being featured in media is a value and a benefit to you. Treat that as a reciprocal relationship.

SECRET MEDIA TIP: DON'T USE THE PHONE.

Not sure why, but entrepreneurs think that calling a station to have a conversation and make a pitch is a valuable strategy. This could not be further from the truth. Don't use the phone. I know a lot of people use phone as a follow-up to their pitch. Written communication works so much better. There are times though when incorporating the phone into your follow up strategy is acceptable. Depending on the outlet, varied communication modes may show strength and persistence, however risky as it could be perceived as negative. An example of this working as part of your follow up strategy is within the power of the initial pitch being written. It is much easier to ask them if they received your email, rather than making a cold call. Utilize this avenue sparingly and not as a primary strategy every time you pitch. The phone does not work well for various reasons. One reason is that you call and leave a message... you have no idea who is checking that message on the other end. Don't assume it's the person you are trying to reach. It could be an assistant or temporary person. If you have been using the phone and not getting results, you may consider eliminating from your strategy immediately.

If you have pitched and followed up a couple of times and still have not heard anything, evaluate your pitch. In most cases there may not be enough value (real or perceived) or you were not interesting enough. You may need to be more strategic in your pitch. Maybe they're on the fence about you a little bit and not quite sold on your pitch. You let a little bit of time go by, rework that pitch, add a little bit more value, and resubmit. Don't just keep following up thinking eventually they will get back with you. Make changes and send a new pitch.

Let's end with briefly examining ROI and media outlets. Most national TV outlets do not pay you to be on their show. Travel expenses are all your responsibility. It's your choice. You make the pitch. You want to be in front of their audience. It's a reciprocal benefit but national TV interviews, national TV shows are, unless you're a high- ranking celebrity, are not going to pay your expenses to get to them. Many get discouraged because they think, oh wow, it's only three minutes. It's only five minutes. The effort and expenses aren't worth a few minutes. This is false. Don't fall prey to this negative, false belief. A lot of people refuse to travel for these. What happens is they miss out on the amazing ROI that comes from being very focused on your strategy [long term] and understanding that ROI comes from elevated credibility which is gained throughout all levels of the process. Speaking of credibility, ROI is not just in the rights to use certain logos. If all you are after are logos, you are missing the boat completely. ROI with the media individually, within the network, the increased credibility towards your audience, the photos that come with social proof, the reels that come from the actual interview, the audience that you're able to get in front of that is already aligned with your target audience, all comes because of the research you did, the increased growth that you will go through, and in the learning of this process. Understanding the psychology behind this process and how you step into a greater version and a stronger version of yourself and your own growth is paramount.

SECRET MEDIA TIP: THE ROI IS NOT ALWAYS WHAT YOU THINK.

Every media outlet offers a different experience with a slightly different way to pitch and build relationships. Working with TV is different than doing a radio interview. Follow this 5- step process for any media outlet that you are working with. If you want to write an article for a magazine, this process is a little bit different. No matter whether a podcast or radio, a Facebook live interview, national television show, or anything that you're being interviewed for, this process works. Again, large print magazine publications are different. For print interviews, you may do an interview via phone or they may email you the questions. If you are pitching to write articles, each major publication has certain requirements and guidelines and you need to research what is needed for each publication.

My final encouragement is to think differently about what that ROI looks like. Opportunity, partnerships, other media appearances, new clients, JV's (Joint Venture's), the social proof, partnerships with higher level players; not to mention your own learning and growth are all available to you. The ROI comes in different ways, but it's amazing, abundant and all around you. Working on your own mindset and how you're thinking, not letting a limiting belief become the factor that keeps you from pitching or from even stepping into this process becomes an amazing motivational factor. The more that you step into this, the more you focus on this, the more you dive into it and figure it out, the faster you can experience major growth. I have helped businesses become transformed through media. The power of media is amazing and will help you get from wherever you are, to where it is that you want to be. Go back and reread this book a thousand times, take more notes, do whatever you need to do, but make this year your best year and incorporate more media strategy into your planning process and overall business strategy. You will experience the benefits that come from doing this. You have my best wishes!

About the Author

Lori McNeil grew up in a creative, hard working family, and that ethic has been with her throughout life. From making barrettes for Christmas bazaars as a first grader, to taking out her first bank loan at age 11 (Lori's mother co-signed with her on $3,500) to start her own hotdog stand, it seems that she's always been reaching for something bigger than herself. It's fair to say that entrepreneurship is woven into the fabric of her life.

As a very young entrepreneur, Lori quickly gained the attention of media. Radio interviews started before she was even open for business. Lori's first live radio remote was 10 minutes in length and ended up being the first of thousands that followed throughout her successful entrepreneurial journey.

Lori has been featured on FOX, NBC, ABC, CBS as well as 500 other media outlets per year. She continues to hone her skills as she trains and coaches other entrepreneurs the power of using media.

As an adult, Lori spent years in education and business, while also being an involved consultant, politician, community advocate and volunteer—both domestically as well as internationally.

Her passion has always been in helping people achieve more success. Helping people achieve their goals is truly what drives Lori! She loves working with people and businesses, guiding them as they seek to achieve higher levels of success in their personal and professional lives. Nothing brings Lori more satisfaction than being there with people when they go from wherever they are, to where they've always wanted to be.

Lori's philosophy is that you need to create and maintain a healthy balance in both your personal and professional life, in order to truly be successful long term. Most people do not understand the significance this has in their life, nor that it is a primary contributor to their achieving success. Well, they don't know what they are missing out on!

Lori loves helping businesses tap into their greatest potential, to shift their mindset, redirect focus and gain greater clarity for their business vision and overall purpose. Business balance is essential for long term success.

Since we don't know what we don't know, Lori strives to help people come to a greater understanding of what it takes to succeed. She loves working with high achievers who are serious about filling in those gaps to deeper understanding, so that we can turn what is unknown into what is known.

Lori coaches and speaks all over the world on a regular basis and continues to reach new levels of success.

Visit https://lorimcneil.com to learn more.

Resources

Appendix A:
The Strategy Behind
Press Releases

Some rules of thumb for press releases.

The press release should be brief, short, and to the point. Longer releases are costly to do, and there are many outlets that you can submit a press release to for free. Do a little bit of research and figure out which ones are free and which ones aren't. There are plenty of both. Trying to get the attention of kind of a bigger outlet cost a bit, but if in your plan, will be worth it.

The Rules

The number one rule is to the point, 400 words or less, broken into two paragraphs is ideal. Rule number two: do not be funny or humorous. Keep it professional. This isn't the place to show your personality and try to build the relationship that way. A mistake that will cost you credibility. This is an opportunity to keep everything value added, very professional and very to the point you. The goal is to 'keep it dry' if you want to think of it that way. The third rule is to proof read it twice. You don't ever want to release anything to any media outlet before you've meticulously checked your spelling and your grammar at a bare minimum. It never hurts to have somebody else to look it over just in case there's something that was missed. The fourth rule with press releases is that you want to target the right media. This is just a reminder because it is something which should continuously be in the forefront of your mind to maintain alignment with your goal, with your vision, with your mission. Only submit press releases after communicating with and/or officially pitching the right media outlets are aligned with what you're trying to accomplish. Randomly submitting press releases or pitches to any media outlet without any strategy means you're not targeting the right audience. When you target the right media outlet that's already aligned with what you're doing, you're targeting your targets. Audiences are going to be the same. Just remember that when you are sending press releases you might not be making an official pitch, but you are introducing yourself and how they see you the first time could lead to a bigger opportunity. You want to make sure that you're in alignment with that. Finally, the fifth rule is to have something valuable to share. It's not just about announcing that you have, say, a book.

What's the value of your book? How can you tie that into a bigger reason of why you are the expert to solve the bigger problem. It is not that you are really an awesome person in your community or state or floating around out there in the nation. What's the purpose of the book? Why should they care? You always want to lead with value. Why is it important that they read this book? How is this book going to help them solve problems? Why are you the expert to help them solve the problem? Some outlets don't like to feature authors because it's not about selling, but that's why you can mention that you're an author. it's about the value that you bring in the problem that you're solving.

When you are building and maintaining your media strategy plan, you want to use press releases, whether locally or in your state or even globally. Remember, you are building your credibility to let people know about your accomplishments, to let them know about an upcoming book, to talk about a cause that's important and why they should care. It's important to start to feature your own accomplishments, your own mission, kind of insert yourself into the overall bigger cause of different organizations. With the right messaging and the right plan, even during the developing phase, you can get noticed. It's okay to communicate that. You can brag on yourself a little bit.

As your business grows, you should have bigger things that you want people to know about. You should have a book or a cause or an event or something, a big award maybe that you've won, or something of the like. You should have ongoing credentials to communicate and to go ahead and let people know about. This strategy is foundational but is also important for maintaining connection and relevance. Finally, if you are using free ways to submit your press release, then leads with value. Who knows who across your state, across the nation, or even globally, might contact you for a further interview? Press releases are an easy way to get the media's attention, provided you give them content that can be used right away. This will also set yourself up for potentially greater media opportunities.

Appendix B:

How Not to be a Bad Guest

You want to make sure that you have your messaging down so clearly so professionally and so on the ball and ready to go, that you are not considered a bad guest. There are things that will automatically put you at the top of the bad guest list pile.

• Providing long answers – 30 seconds or less. Now the only way that this might be a little bit longer than 30 seconds is if you are on an hour podcast. You will be going back and forth in a fluid conversation. And there's many questions where you can give longer answers. Most podcasts are going to be anywhere from anywhere from 20 to 60 minutes. Your research and during your pitch process and the acceptance and invitation process, you should find out how long of a timeframe your segment is, or the show is. That will help you to kind of gauge the length of your answers a little bit. Television or shorter podcasts, you should only practice giving 30 second answers. Talking fluff and not getting to the point will end you up as

being a bad guest if you end up getting too long of answers.

• Giving too complex of answers. You want to speak
simply. Radio interviews, for example, are not college
lectures, and your goal is not to tell the audience everything you know about the topic. Don't give too much data, don't give too much statistics, don't give too much
information. Don't try to prove everything you know in
every single answer. That's not the goal. Make sure that
your answers are very simple, short, brief, and to the
point.

• Do not be boring. Radio especially requires energy,
but any type of an interview really requires energy. You
should be interesting in the way that you move your body
and in your facial expressions. If it happens to be on a live
video feed or on a live, you know, broadcast on TV, you
must be full of energy, you must be interesting. Don't be
so nervous that you're so stoic and so boring. Therefore,
practicing is vitally important. Practice in the mirror and
you want to watch your movements. You want to pay attention to your facial expressions and how you use and
move your body and how you use your hands when you
talk. Those elements are super important. Too many
guests put a premium on the quality of their information
on not nearly enough on the delivery of it. You want to
make sure that you are coming across well. If you're adding complete value, great information, it's going to be
easy for them to even listen to what you have to say.

• The BIG thing that makes you a bad guest is if you're
an alarmist. Who wants to hear someone tell us that their

life is terrible and that you're doomed to suffer, and every problem has a solution, and everyone should want to know what it is? If your attitude is that there are no solutions, people will tune out. And if you're making your audience feel like everything, they're doing is wrong because you're pointing out that there not recycling enough or they're not healthy enough and they're not exercising enough, you lose credibility. You don't want your messaging to be negative. Never invoke negative energy which will produce a negative emotion. It's not all doom and gloom or hopeless.

• The final of the top five things that bad guests do is that they leave their humor behind. It's okay to show your personality. It's okay to tell a little bit of a joke or a little bit of a funny story and be personable. You want to do that. You want to connect with them personally. You want to show emotion. You want people to feel that emotion and feel connected to you. Some formats are lighter than others. Every different host has a different personality of course, and you want to be yourself, but you want to make sure that you're keeping in tone with the host and with the tone of the show at the same time. Nothing is worse for a humorous host than a guest who refuses to play along. I was on the radio not that long ago where the host was just cracking up jokes right and left. It wasn't natural for me to throw back very many jokes continually. I had to adjust, and I had to up my humor game and I had to keep with the tone of the host and the show that he had created. If I didn't do that, he wouldn't ask me back. He wouldn't refer me, he wouldn't represent me. He wouldn't and it wouldn't have been a very fun show.

It would have completely killed his audience and hurt his show, hurt his branding. It would've hurt me because I would have looked boring compared to him. You have to kind of match that a little bit. If you have a show that likes to be funny, feel free to be funny back or throw in an extra joke or so it adds interest to the show, especially if that's the overall tone of the show and of the audience anyway.

There you have it: the five things that create a bad guest. Do not to be a bad guest!

Worksheets

These worksheets are a little difficult to read in a 6" x 9" book, so I have made them available for download on my website. Please visit www.lorimcneil.com/worksheets

PRE-PLANNING

This video discusses the importance of pre planning as a vital part of the 5-strategy process BEFORE you actually make a pitch. To best evaluate what needs to be improved in order to be more prepared, we need to establish what your on and off line presence currently looks like.

Please list ALL your online social media platforms, including websites, that you are currently using, both personal and professional.

Website: _____ What needs improved? _____

Facebook: _____ What needs improved? _____

Twitter: _____ What needs improved? _____

Instagram: _____ What needs improved? _____

LinkedIn: _____ What needs improved? _____

Other: _____ What needs improved? _____

In order to maintain clear messaging and branding on ALL platforms, they all need the same fonts, colors, images etc.... which platforms need work and what aspects need to be improved?

Now that you have your on and offline presence in order, you need to identify the media outlets that best align with you and your messaging.

After you have taken ample time to research outlets, you need to make a list of the first 5, either local or national, that you will pitch. Write down 5 outlets that you WILL pitch over the next 30 days.

Media Outlet & Location #1: _____

Media Influencers Identified: _____

Emails for each Influencer: _____

Media Outlet & Location #2: _____

Media Influencers Identified: _____

Emails for each Influencer: _____

Media Outlet & Location #3: _____

Media Influencers Identified: _____

Emails for each Influencer: _____

Media Outlet & Location #4: _____

Media Influencers Identified: _____

Emails for each Influencer: _____

In addition, make notes on any other "aha" moments you had during this training or new ideas that you don't want to forget.

_____

_____

_____

_____

What was best tip you learned about pitching? Write it down here so you can refer back to it later.

_____

_____

_____

_____

PITCH

During this second training, you will begin to understand the important aspects of Pitch. This aspects in this strategy are often overlooked or not taken seriously. This is either because of a lack of knowledge or a lack of experience. Even when the 4 main components of the pitch seem simple, they hold much power. Don't be afraid to try new strategies or make slight differences to those 4 components you have already tried. Sometimes small changes can yield big results.

It is important to acknowledge what you have tried to this point and evaluate a new plan. Literally seeing this infor- mation on paper in front of you can make a huge difference in how you process the information and execute a plan for moving forward.

Make a list of the top 3 strategies you have tried or are currently trying when pitching to media. Be sure and include email, messenger, chat bots, phone, make a list of your top 3 strategies.

1. Pitch Strategy:

What's Working

What's not working?

2. Pitch Strategy:

What's Working?

What's not working?

3.) Pitch Strategy:

What's Working?

What's not working?

Now that you have a list in front you what you have been doing, you are going to make a list of your new or slightly different pitch strategies that you are going to implement to create 3 brand new pitch strategies for your new plan.

Again, these may be slightly improved from the list you made above, or they may be completely different.

1.) NEW Pitch Strategy:

2.) NEW Pitch Strategy:

3.) NEW Pitch Strategy:

Now that you have 3 clear pitch strategies, you need to identify which outlets you will begin pitching to using your new plan. Be sure and include which of the 2 pitch types you will need to pitch each media outlet.

In addition, make notes on any other "aha" moments you had during this training or new ideas that you don't want to forget.

What was best tip you learned about pitching?

Write it down here so you can refer back to it later.

PREPARATION

During this training, we are going to assume you have an accepted pitch and now you need to prepare for your actual interview. The preparation is the same whether you will be interviewed on a radio station, TV, FB LIVE or Podcast.

There are a few differences for a magazine interview. However, for the purposes of our training, we will focus on the interviews where you will be speaking that are not in print format.

There is a part of the preparation that takes place during the pre-planning phase. However, the preparation that we will now focus on is the preparation needed AFTER your pitch has been accepted and BEFORE your actual scheduled interview takes place.

When you have been officially accepted and invited for an interview, you are given more details about logistics and how to best prepare. No matter how much information you have been provided, you still have many things you need to do to prepare and maximize your opportunity.

Based on the information you have been provided and the additional information you have learned, fill out the following information for your interview.

Name of Media Outlet: _____ Location: _____

Address: _____

Contact Name: _____ Name of segment: _____

Host(s) name (s): _____

Time allotted for your segment: _____

Type   of   Interview:_____
Are you allowed to sell anything? If so, what are you selling?

_____

 3-5 Main talking points:

_____
_____
_____
_____
_____

Colors and set design or format: _____

Will you have a book or other props? _____

In addition, make notes on any other "aha" moments you had during this training or new ideas that you don't want to forget.

What was best tip you learned about preparation?

Write it down here so you can refer back to it later.

PERFORMANCE

This is the strategy that requires you to practice and perfect your actual interview. A lot of entrepreneurs make the mistake of not practicing because they think they know their material well or that maybe they have spoken on stage or in groups, so they don't need the practice. Do not make that vital mistake. Practicing your messaging and your nonverbal communication is essential. Remember that time goes by faster than you think during any interview, so you need to be fully prepared to answer any question with clarity and consistency.

Write down the details of your Practice Plan. It will help you to stay focused and hold yourself accountable. You will need to duplicate this process for each outlet you are scheduled for.

Date of your Interview:

Time Allotted:

WILL you practice using video or audio only?

How many days per week will you practice?

How many minutes each session WILL you dedicate to practicing?

After each practice session or week (depending on how much time you have), make notes on what challenges you are facing. Do you stumble over your words? Too many "ums" and "likes?" Are your answers too long? Are your answers interesting? Are you having trouble staying with the allotted time? How is your body language?

List your challenges still needing work:

_____

_____

_____

In addition, make notes on any other "aha" moments you had during this training or new ideas that you don't want to forget.

Media Notes:

_____

_____

_____

_____

What was best tip you learned about Performance? Write it down here so you can refer back to it later.

_____

_____

_____

_____

POST-PLANNING

A lot of entrepreneurs and influencers drop the ball on this final strategy. Whether your pitch has been accepted or not, this step must not be skipped. It goes beyond a follow up email.

How you proceed through the Post-Planning process is vital to networking, relationships, credibility, and over brand building. It could also determine whether you get considered in the future or get asked to come back. Do not skip this step!

If you are like most entrepreneurs, you may send a quick "thank you email" or make a few tags on social media. This is great but it's not enough to really put yourself above all the other noise out there that allows you to really stand out and be remembered. You want to make a solid impression and be remembered, whether you get the interview or not.

If your pitch is not accepted, it doesn't mean that it won't be in the future, so you still want to build the relationship and keep communication lines open. If this happens, send a "thank you for your consideration" type of email; short and sweet but most of all, professional.

If your pitch was accepted and you have completed your interview, then you really need to show appreciation and continue building that relationship and credibility!

Below is a short checklist you can use after each interview to make sure you are not skipping this step and ensuring that some key strategies are completed.

Post Planning Checklist:

▶ Along with a thank you email; you want to also send a hand- written card in the mail that includes photos if possible.

▶ Social media posts immediately following each interview with tags to key influencers associated with that specific outlet.

▶ Make several posts with different photos over the next week.

▶ Send Facebook friend request or follow professional pages of those influencers you met and had contact with during your interview.

▶Send personal Facebook or other social media private messages to those key influencers thanking them for the opportunity and mentioning something specific or personal that was shared or discussed to continue the personal relationship building with each key person of influence.

▶ Add value to the main outlets media pages by interacting, making connections beneficial to THEM and adding value to THEM and their stories- NOT YOURS. Continue doing this on a regular basis at least 1-2 times per week. Let them see you and notice you more and discover that you care about adding value and not just being on their show and using them to meet your needs.

If you have additional Post-Planning strategies that are specific to your messaging and industry, list those additional strategies here:

_____

_____

In addition, make notes on any other "aha" moments you had during this training or new ideas that you don't want to forget.

Media Notes:

_____

_____

What was best tip you learned about Post-Planning? Write it down here so you can refer back to it later.

www.ingramcontent.com/pod-product-compliance
Lightning Source LLC
Chambersburg PA
CBHW060625210326
41520CB00010B/1476